GRAPHIC FORENSIC SCIENCE

AUTOPSIES:
PATHOLOGISTS AT WORK

by Gary Jeffrey

illustrated by Terry Riley

FRANKLIN WATTS
LONDON•SYDNEY

First published in 2009 by Franklin Watts

Franklin Watts
338 Euston Road
London NW1 3BH

Franklin Watts Australia
Level 17/207 Kent Street
Sydney, NSW 2000

A CIP catalogue record for this book is available from the British Library.

Dewey number: 363.2'562

ISBN: 978 0 7496 9245 2

Franklin Watts is a division of Hachette Children's Books,
an Hachette UK company.
www.hachette.co.uk

GRAPHIC FORENSIC SCIENCE: AUTOPSIES produced for Franklin Watts by David
West Children's Books, 7 Princeton Court, 55 Felsham Road, London SW15 1AZ

Designed and produced by
David West Children's Books

Editor: Gail Bushnell

Photo credits:
4&5, Rich Legg; 6t&6m, New York City Medical Examiner's Collection, National
Museum of Health and Medicine, Armed Forces Institute of Pathology, Washington,
D.C., 6b, Ryan Roberts; 44b, Duncan P. Walker.

Printed in China

Website disclaimer:
Note to parents and teachers: Every effort has been made by the Publishers to ensure
that the websites in this book are suitable for children, that they are of the highest
educational value, and that they contain no inappropriate or offensive material.
However, because of the nature of the Internet, it is impossible to guarantee that the
contents of these sites will not be altered. We strongly advise that the Internet is
supervised by a responsible adult.

CONTENTS

SCENE OF THE CRIME

Forensics is the examination of physical evidence to be presented in a court of law. At the scene of a crime the forensic scientist who examines the dead body is called a pathologist.

COLLECTING EVIDENCE

The pathologist is often also the coroner at a crime scene and is the person in charge of the crime scene investigators (CSI). In the UK these investigators are called scene of crime officers (SOCO). CSI are civilians and police officers specially trained as evidence technicians. While the CSI photograph and gather evidence the pathologist focuses on the body.

The pathologist is particularly interested in the position of the corpse, any obvious wounding and any material evidence located on or near the body - anything, in fact, that may give early clues as to the time and cause of death. Eventually the body is taken to a mortuary for a more thorough examination, called a post-mortem.

How is the body lying? Is there a possible murder weapon nearby? Are there any obviously fatal wounds? Is there any obvious evidence to indicate time of death? These are the questions in a pathologist's mind when first approaching a crime scene.

POST-MORTEM EXAM

The post-mortem dissection, or autopsy, was first developed during the Renaissance to investigate violent deaths. It is still the main method used by forensic pathologists to determine the cause of suspicious deaths today.

A DIALOGUE WITH THE DEAD

When examining a body, the pathologist aims to place the manner of death in one of five categories: **natural**, **accidental**, **homicide**, **suicide** or **undetermined**. The first step is to look at the surface of the body and note any remarkable physical features and trace evidence. Next, the body is opened with surgical instruments and organs are removed and sliced (sectioned) so that they can be examined more closely under a microscope. Bodily fluids and tissues are taken and tested using chemical analysis.

These tools enable the pathologist to work like a medical detective, gathering the evidence needed to reconstruct the mechanism of death.

425
PENETRATING STAB WOUND OF
KIDNEY.
HOMICIDAL.

Sectioning of internal organs, like this kidney, can reveal the depth of a stab wound and whether it was fatal.

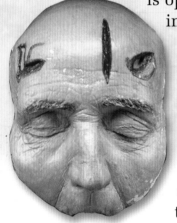

A visual aid from 1965 showing different wound characteristics.

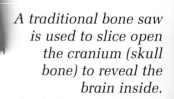

A traditional bone saw is used to slice open the cranium (skull bone) to reveal the brain inside.

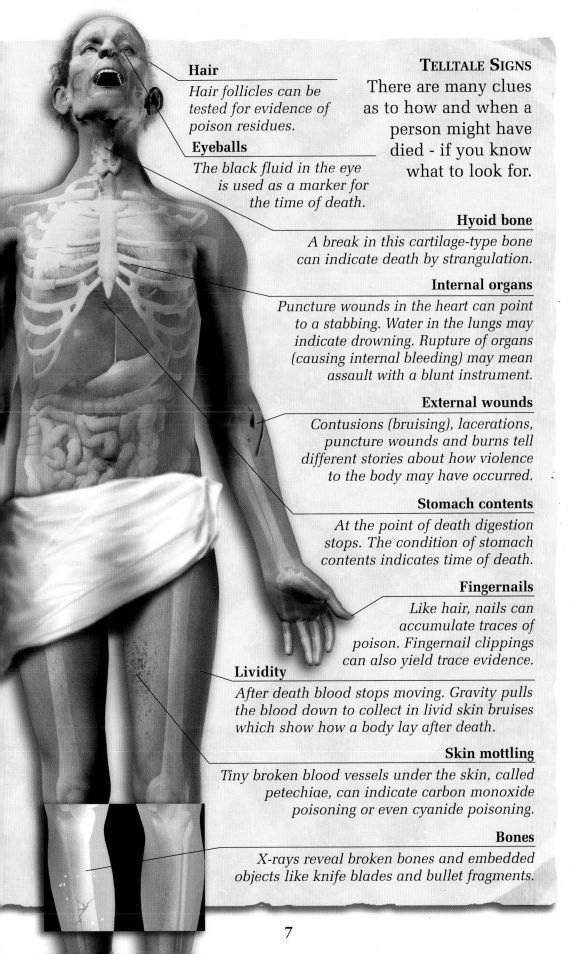

Hair

Hair follicles can be tested for evidence of poison residues.

Eyeballs

The black fluid in the eye is used as a marker for the time of death.

There are many clues as to how and when a person might have died - if you know what to look for.

Hyoid bone

A break in this cartilage-type bone can indicate death by strangulation.

Internal organs

Puncture wounds in the heart can point to a stabbing. Water in the lungs may indicate drowning. Rupture of organs (causing internal bleeding) may mean assault with a blunt instrument.

External wounds

Contusions (bruising), lacerations, puncture wounds and burns tell different stories about how violence to the body may have occurred.

Stomach contents

At the point of death digestion stops. The condition of stomach contents indicates time of death.

Fingernails

Like hair, nails can accumulate traces of poison. Fingernail clippings can also yield trace evidence.

Lividity

After death blood stops moving. Gravity pulls the blood down to collect in livid skin bruises which show how a body lay after death.

Skin mottling

Tiny broken blood vessels under the skin, called petechiae, can indicate carbon monoxide poisoning or even cyanide poisoning.

Bones

X-rays reveal broken bones and embedded objects like knife blades and bullet fragments.

THE BODY IN THE BASEMENT

KENNINGTON LANE, VAUXHALL, LONDON, 17 JULY 1942.

TWO YEARS EARLIER, DURING THE HEIGHT OF THE BLITZ*, THE CHAPEL HAD TAKEN A DIRECT HIT. IT WAS ONLY NOW BEING DEMOLISHED.

CAN YOU GIVE US A HAND WITH THIS SLAB, ROLY?

WHEW, I'LL BE GLAD WHEN WE GET THIS LEVELLED.

HEY!

*THE BOMBING OF LONDON IN WORLD WAR II.

OKAY NOW, EASY DOES... HEY, WHAT'S THAT?

OH NO, NOT ANOTHER ONE!

OLD AIR RAID VICTIM?

COULD BE. LET ME GET MY...

BLIMEY! I THINK WE'D BETTER CALL THE POLICE!

LATER, AT SOUTHWARK MORTUARY...

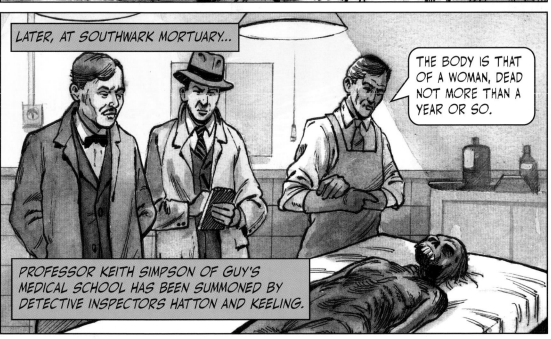

THE BODY IS THAT OF A WOMAN, DEAD NOT MORE THAN A YEAR OR SO.

PROFESSOR KEITH SIMPSON OF GUY'S MEDICAL SCHOOL HAS BEEN SUMMONED BY DETECTIVE INSPECTORS HATTON AND KEELING.

THE HEAD HAS BEEN SEVERED AND HAD FLESH SCRAPED FROM THE FACE.

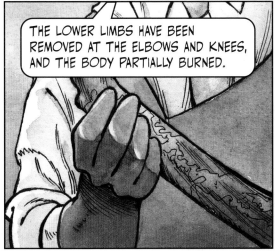

THE LOWER LIMBS HAVE BEEN REMOVED AT THE ELBOWS AND KNEES, AND THE BODY PARTIALLY BURNED.

9

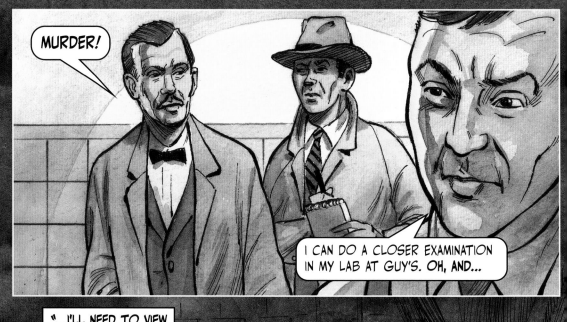

MURDER!

I CAN DO A CLOSER EXAMINATION IN MY LAB AT GUY'S. OH, AND...

"...I'LL NEED TO VIEW THE GRAVE SITE..."

NO TRACE OF THE MISSING LIMBS, BUT LOOK AT THIS YELLOW SOIL.

LIME?

USED TO MASK THE STENCH OF PUTREFACTION, NO DOUBT.

WHOEVER DID THIS DIDN'T WANT THE BODY FOUND RIGHT AWAY.

NEXT DAY, PATHOLOGY DEPARTMENT, GUY'S MEDICAL SCHOOL...

OBSERVE HOW THE BROW PLATES ARE COMPLETELY FUSED.

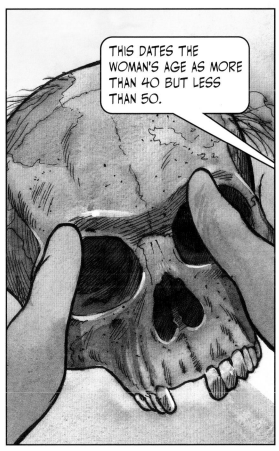

THIS DATES THE WOMAN'S AGE AS MORE THAN 40 BUT LESS THAN 50.

LOWER JAW IS MISSING, BUT THE UPPER JAW BEARS THE MARKS OF A DENTAL PLATE...

...AND THERE ARE ALSO FILLINGS IN THE TEETH.

ALL EVIDENCE THAT CAN BE MATCHED TO THE DENTAL RECORDS OF A MISSING PERSON.

11

12

HERE WE ARE... RACHEL DOBKIN, AGED 49. REPORTED MISSING 12 APRIL 1941...

"...BY HER SISTER."

THE LAST PERSON TO SEE RACHEL WAS THAT WRETCHED HUSBAND OF HERS.

HARRY DOBKIN?

YES, I TOLD THE POLICE TO TALK TO HIM THE DAY AFTER SHE WENT MISSING. BUT THEY NEVER DID.

MISS DUBINSKI, WOULD YOU HAVE THE NAME OF RACHEL'S DENTIST?

13

A. KOPKIN—

ENTIST

YES, THAT'S HER JAW. NO DOUBT ABOUT IT!

WITH THE VICTIM NOW KNOWN, POLICE CAN INTERVIEW WITNESSES AND GATHER INFORMATION.

A FEW WEEKS LATER HATTON AND KEELING PRESENT THEIR CASE TO THE CHIEF SUPERINTENDENT...

SO, THE DOBKINS WERE MARRIED FOR ONLY THREE DAYS AND THEN LIVED APART FOR MORE THAN 20 YEARS?

YES, CHIEF, AND IT SEEMS HARRY WAS ANGRY AT HAVING TO CONTINUE PAYING ALIMONY FOR THEIR NOW 20-YEAR-OLD SON...

...PLUS HE WAS A FIRE WARDEN IN THE PREMISES NEXT DOOR TO THE BOMBED-OUT CHURCH.

A FEW MONTHS AFTER RACHEL WENT MISSING WITNESSES SAW HIM PUTTING OUT A SMALL FIRE IN THE CRYPT.

HARRY DOBKIN IS TAKEN TO THE CRYPT. HE IS QUESTIONED, BUT DENIES ANY INVOLVEMENT IN HIS WIFE'S DEATH.

IT SEEMED STRANGE BECAUSE THERE HAD BEEN NO RAIDS FOR A WHILE.

SHORTLY AFTER, HE IS ARRESTED AND CHARGED WITH HER MURDER.

THE PROSECUTOR IN THE CASE IS CONFIDENT OF A CONVICTION, EXCEPT...

...IF THERE'S ANY DOUBT AT ALL ABOUT THE VICTIM'S IDENTITY, THE CASE COULD COLLAPSE.

I'LL SEE WHAT I CAN DO.

AUTUMN 1942. PROFESSOR SIMPSON GIVES EVIDENCE AT THE TRIAL OF HARRY DOBKIN.

TO BE SURE OF THE VICTIM'S IDENTITY WE PHOTOGRAPHED THE REMAINS OF THE SKULL...

...AND SUPERIMPOSED IT ON A PHOTOGRAPH OF RACHEL DOBKIN.

AS YOU CAN SEE, THE MATCH IS QUITE REMARKABLE.

THE JURY TAKES 20 MINUTES TO FIND HARRY DOBKIN GUILTY.

HE IS SENTENCED TO **HANG**.

BEFORE HIS EXECUTION DOBKIN CONFESSES TO KILLING RACHEL. HE WAS SICK OF BEING PESTERED FOR MONEY. HE THOUGHT HE COULD DISGUISE THE BODY TO LOOK LIKE AN AIR RAID VICTIM.

PROFESSOR KEITH SIMPSON WENT ON TO WRITE THE FIRST STUDENT TEXTBOOK ON FORENSIC SCIENCE. IT IS STILL IN PRINT TODAY.

THE END

TIME OF DEATH

SEPTEMBER 1983, NYACK, NEW YORK. DETECTIVE MIKE YOUNGMAN HAS CALLED IN CHIEF MEDICAL EXAMINER FREDERICK ZUGIBE TO EXAMINE A GRUESOME DISCOVERY...

FIRST THING - IT DOESN'T SMELL RIGHT.

CLICK!

ZZZZZZZZZZZZZZZ

YEAH, I KNOW WHAT YOU MEAN.

CLICK!

BUGS DON'T SEEM TO MIND IT, THOUGH.

THIS ONE IS GOING TO BE A PUZZLE.

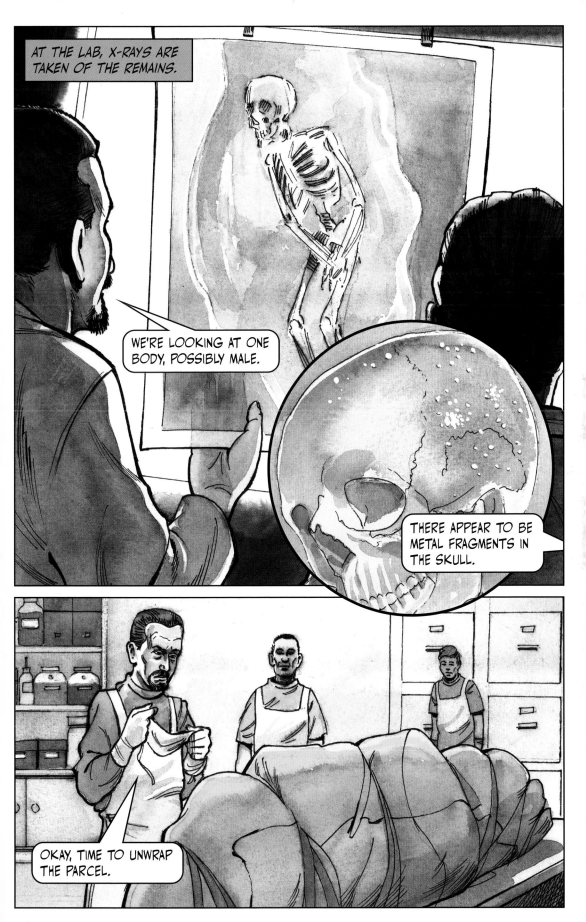

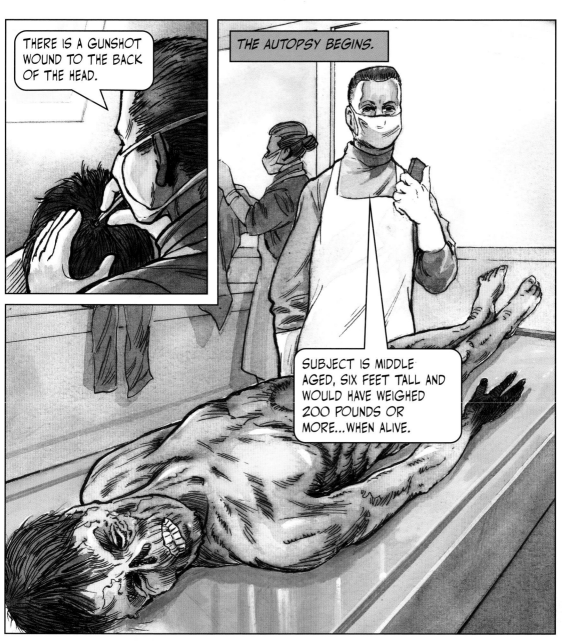

THERE IS A GUNSHOT WOUND TO THE BACK OF THE HEAD.

THE AUTOPSY BEGINS.

SUBJECT IS MIDDLE AGED, SIX FEET TALL AND WOULD HAVE WEIGHED 200 POUNDS OR MORE...WHEN ALIVE.

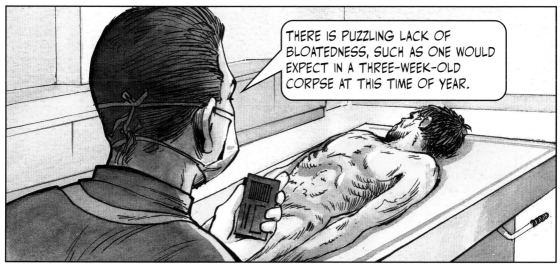

THERE IS PUZZLING LACK OF BLOATEDNESS, SUCH AS ONE WOULD EXPECT IN A THREE-WEEK-OLD CORPSE AT THIS TIME OF YEAR.

THE SKIN HAS A STRANGE GREASY TEXTURE THAT I'VE NEVER SEEN BEFORE.

THE SKIN IS ALSO A REMARKABLE BEIGE PUTTY COLOUR...MOST ODD.

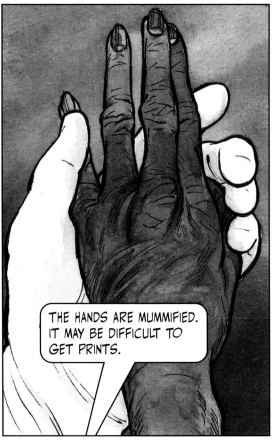

THE HANDS ARE MUMMIFIED. IT MAY BE DIFFICULT TO GET PRINTS.

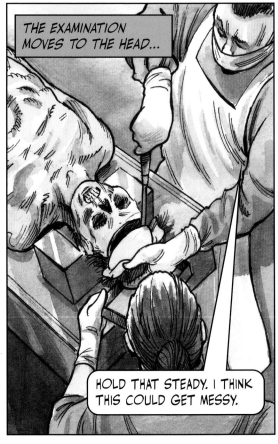

THE EXAMINATION MOVES TO THE HEAD...

HOLD THAT STEADY. I THINK THIS COULD GET MESSY.

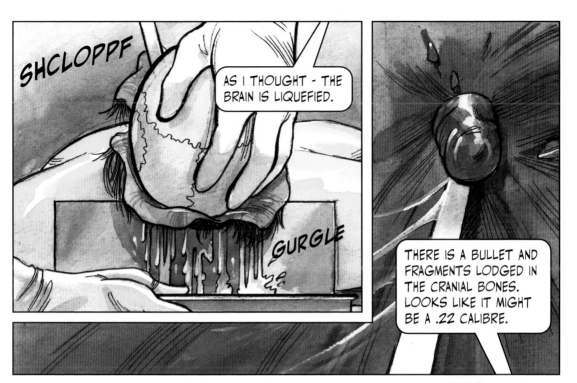

SHCLOPPF

AS I THOUGHT – THE BRAIN IS LIQUEFIED.

GURGLE

THERE IS A BULLET AND FRAGMENTS LODGED IN THE CRANIAL BONES. LOOKS LIKE IT MIGHT BE A .22 CALIBRE.

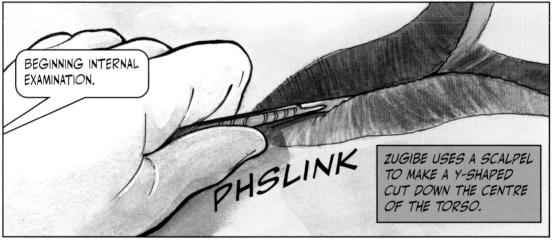

BEGINNING INTERNAL EXAMINATION.

PHSLINK

ZUGIBE USES A SCALPEL TO MAKE A Y-SHAPED CUT DOWN THE CENTRE OF THE TORSO.

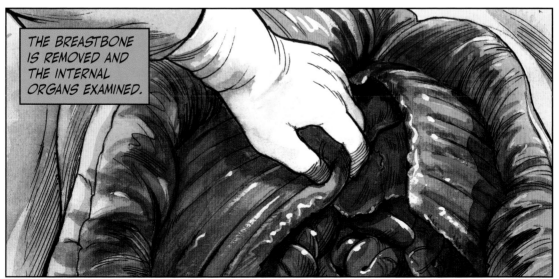

THE BREASTBONE IS REMOVED AND THE INTERNAL ORGANS EXAMINED.

I'VE NEVER SEEN ANYTHING LIKE THIS. THE OUTSIDE OF THE BODY IS PULPY AND FORMLESS, YET THESE ORGANS ARE WELL PRESERVED.

IT'S AS IF THE NORMAL PROCESS OF DECOMPOSITION HAS BEEN TOTALLY REVERSED.

USUALLY THE INSIDES WOULD BE THE FIRST PARTS TO BREAK DOWN.

WHEN THE AUTOPSY IS FINISHED THE HEART AND OTHER ORGANS ARE SECTIONED AND STORED.

SOMETHING'S HAPPENED TO THIS BODY THAT'S DISTORTED THE FORENSIC EVIDENCE, BUT WHAT?...AND WHY?

ZUGIBE IS PUZZLED. HOWEVER, WHEN HE IS DRIVING HOME A FEW DAYS LATER...

FERMAN'S FROZEN FOOD SERVICE

HMM...FERMAN'S FROZEN FOOD SERVICES...

...WAIT, THAT'S IT!

I'VE GOT TO GET BACK TO THE LAB!

SCREEECH!

25

ZUGIBE SEARCHES OUT SOME TISSUE SAMPLES TAKEN FROM THE JOHN DOE'S HEART...

AHA! JUST AS I THOUGHT!

NEXT DAY HE CALLS THE POLICE...

SERIOUSLY? YOU THINK THIS GUY'S CORPSE IS TWO YEARS OLD?

YES, AND I CAN PROVE IT!

HEY, MIKE! OUR MEDICAL EXAMINER THINKS HE'S DR QUINCY*!

HEH, HEH!

*THE BRILLIANT, FICTIONAL TV MEDICAL EXAMINER.

26

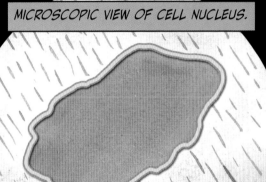

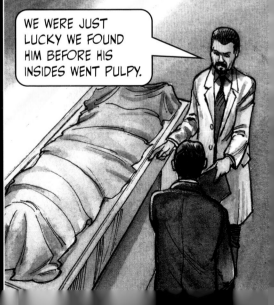

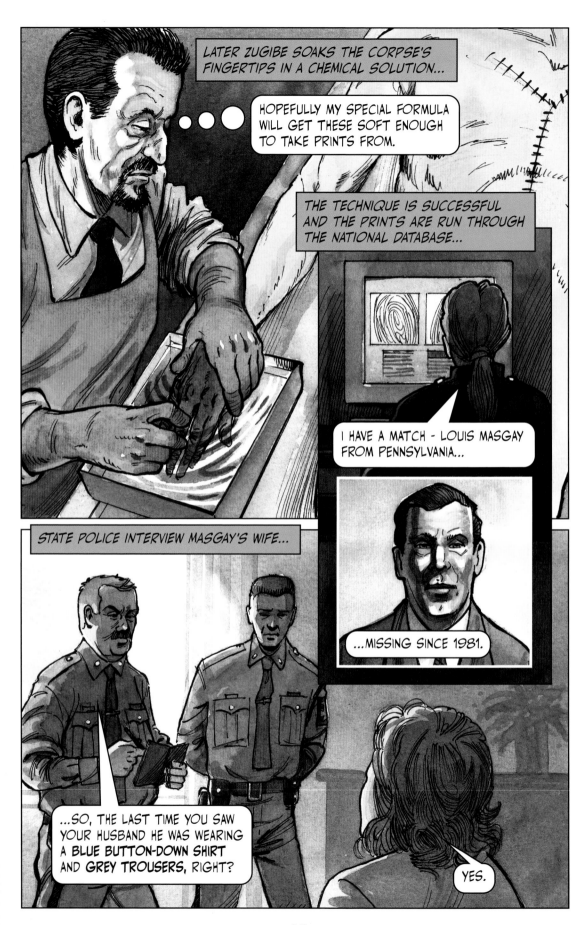

HE WAS GOING TO A BUSINESS MEETING IN NEW JERSEY BUT HE NEVER CAME HOME.

WOULD YOU HAVE THE NAME OF THE MAN HE WAS GOING TO MEET?

THE MAN, *RICHARD KUKLINSKI*, IS ALREADY UNDER INVESTIGATION BY THE FBI AND NEW JERSEY STATE POLICE...

...FOR THE MURDER OF THESE TWO CAR THIEVES, GARY SMITH AND DANIEL DEPPNER.

DEPPNER WAS FOUND NEAR A RANCH IN WEST MILFORD...

...WRAPPED IN **GREEN** GARBAGE BAGS.

POLICE DEPT
CUMONT, NJ
RICHARD KUI...
CB2-09

KUKLINSKI, NICKNAMED 'THE ICEMAN', IS A SCAM ARTIST AND SUSPECTED MAFIA HIT MAN. HE BECOMES SUSPECT NUMBER ONE. HOWEVER, THERE IS NO EVIDENCE TO LINK HIM *DIRECTLY* TO MASGAY'S MURDER.

ONE TIME THEY FOUND THIS GUY UP IN ROCKLAND. THEY FIGURED OUT HE'D BEEN DEAD FOR TWO AND A HALF WEEKS...

...ONLY HE'D **REALLY** BEEN DEAD TWO AND A HALF YEARS!

YEAH?

COLD STORE

YEAH, IN THE DEEP FREEZE *NOTHING* CHANGES.

IT'S JUST LIKE PULLING OUT A **STEAK**.

RICHARD KUKLINSKI IS ARRESTED AND CHARGED. IT TAKES FIVE OFFICERS TO PULL HIM IN.

LATER A PRISONER, PHILIP SOLIMENE, TESTIFIES THAT HE SAW A CORPSE RESEMBLING LOUIS MASGAY...

...HANGING IN THE FREEZER COMPARTMENT OF KUKLINSKI'S WAREHOUSE IN 1982.

ROCKLAND, 1998...

"KUKLINSKI HAS BEEN A PROFESSIONAL KILLER FOR THE BETTER PART OF TWO DECADES, TAKING OVER 100 LIVES IN AS MANY DIFFERENT WAYS."

ICEMAN MELTS

WELL, IT SEEMS OUR MR. MASGAY WAS SIMPLY AN EXPERIMENT IN BODY DISPOSAL!

KUKLINSKI WOULD HAVE GOTTEN AWAY WITH IT, TOO, IF HE HADN'T WRAPPED THE BODY UP SO...*PROFESSIONALLY!*

DR FREDERICK T. ZUGIBE RETIRED IN 2003 AFTER A DISTINGUISHED CAREER, DURING WHICH HE PUBLISHED MANY PAPERS *AND* A BEST-SELLING BOOK.

RICHARD KUKLINSKI WAS CONVICTED OF FIVE MURDERS. ALTHOUGH LACK OF EYEWITNESS TESTIMONY SPARED HIM THE DEATH PENALTY HE WAS SENTENCED TO TWO LIFE TERMS...

...TO BE SERVED BACK TO BACK.

IN 2006...

KUKLINSKI, RICHARD, DEATH BY UNKNOWN CAUSES. OKAY, LET'S STICK HIM IN THE FREEZER.

THE END

THE PENNSYLVANIA POISONING
MYSTERY

AUGUST, 1991. CONTRACTOR ROBERT CURLEY IS HELPING RENOVATE A LABORATORY AT WILKES UNIVERSITY, PENNSYLVANIA WHEN...

AAAAGH! MY SKIN IS BURNING!

MUWAGH....MUWAGH...

BWEEEEARGH!

LATER, AT WILKES-BARRE HOSPITAL...

MRS CURLEY, PLEASE BE PATIENT, WE'RE DOING EVERYTHING WE CAN...

BURNING SKIN, WEAKNESS, VOMITING AND RAPID HAIR LOSS - ANY IDEAS?

HE HAS A NORMAL THYROID AND HASN'T BEEN EXPOSED TO RADIATION - FRANKLY, I'M STUMPED!

IT'S GOOD THAT HE'S SLOWLY IMPROVING...

CURLEY'S HEALTH IMPROVES ENOUGH FOR HIM TO GO HOME.

HOWEVER, A FEW WEEKS LATER...

OH, PLEASE, COME QUICKLY! BOB'S SICK AGAIN AND THIS TIME HE'S ACTING REALLY WEIRD!

GAAAAURRGH

FROM HIS AGGRESSIVE BEHAVIOUR I THINK WE HAVE TO SUSPECT HEAVY METAL POISONING.

CURLEY HAS BEEN TRANSFERRED TO THE HERSHEY MEDICAL CENTER AT PENN STATE.

NNNNNYAAAAGH!

BETTER SCREEN HIM FOR TOXINS.

HE'S SHOWING HIGH LEVELS OF **THALLIUM.**

WOW, THAT STUFF'S LETHAL!

THEY USED TO USE IT IN RAT POISON, BUT IT WAS OUTLAWED IN '84.

SO HOW DID THALLIUM GET INSIDE THIS GUY?

36

WHILE JOANN CURLEY AND HER DAUGHTER ARE TESTED FOR THALLIUM, THE CURLEY HOME IS SEARCHED...

THE ONLY THING WE CAN FIND THAT'S HAD THALLIUM IN IT IS THIS THERMOS.

THE TOXICOLOGY LAB SAYS MRS CURLEY AND HER DAUGHTER BOTH HAVE THALLIUM IN THEIR SYSTEMS.

HE USED IT FOR HIS ICED TEA, BUT I'VE NO IDEA HOW ANYTHING COULD HAVE GOTTEN IN THERE FROM THE HOUSE.

WHEN JOANN CURLEY SUES THE UNIVERSITY FOR WRONGFUL DEATH, THE POLICE BECOME SUSPICIOUS...

DISTRICT ATT

TWO DAYS BEFORE BOB CURLEY DIED SHE COLLECTED OVER $1 MILLION FOR THE WRONGFUL DEATH OF HER *PREVIOUS* HUSBAND IN AN AUTO ACCIDENT.

THE ELEVATED LEVELS OF THALLIUM BEGIN NINE MONTHS *BEFORE* HE STARTED WORKING AT THE UNIVERSITY.

IF YOU LOOK AT THE SPIKES IN THALLIUM LEVELS, IT'S PRETTY OBVIOUS THAT MR CURLEY...

...WAS BEING SYSTEMATICALLY POISONED!

CYRIL WECHT SUMS IT UP...

WHAT WE NEED TO DO NOW IS TO COMPARE THIS WITH A TIMETABLE OF BOB CURLEY'S MOVEMENTS IN HIS LAST YEAR OF LIFE...

...AND IF YOU PUT THE CHARTS SIDE BY SIDE YOU CAN SEE THAT WHENEVER CURLEY WAS AWAY FROM HIS WIFE...

...AWAY ON BUSINESS, SAY, OR IN THE HOSPITAL...

...HIS THALLIUM LEVELS WENT DOWN.

EXCEPT TWO DAYS BEFORE THE END, WHEN THIS SPIKE SHOWS A MASSIVE INGESTION - THE FATAL DOSE.

COULD YOU PASS ME THOSE WITNESS STATEMENTS?

OTHER FAMOUS CASES

Here are some other celebrated cases that relied on the science of pathology to help solve a crime.

THE DEAD MAN'S GRIP

1855, Lyon, France. In the bed of a locked room an old man lay dead from a gunshot to the head. In his hand was a revolver. To Professor Alexandre Lacassagne it looked like an obvious case of suicide, except there were oddities.

The bedclothes had been pulled up over the man's arms, surely impossible to do after being shot in the head? Also, where were the telltale powder burns around the entrance wound from the close-range shot? Lacassagne suspected the 'suicide' had been staged, except how could a dead man's hand have been made to grip the pistol? Lacassagne decided to find out through an experiment.

He placed an object loosely in the hand of a freshly dead hospital corpse. After a few hours, as rigor mortis set in, the hand closed tightly around the object, as if gripping it. The old man's son was questioned and confessed to his murder. Lacassagne had solved the crime using his knowledge of 'death's clock'.

THE RUXTON 'JIGSAW' MURDER

In 1935 scattered packages containing over 70 dismembered body parts were found in a river in Scotland. The task of assembling this human jigsaw puzzle fell to Professor Jon Glaister and a team of forensic pathologists.

They quickly discovered they were dealing with two female bodies that had been carefully jointed using a knife. Such precision required surgical skill - could the murderer be a doctor? The bodies' ages were determined - the larger woman over 40, the younger in her 20s.

The older woman seemed to have been murdered in a fit of rage. The younger, beaten with a heavy object, had probably been a witness. The case was cracked when a wrapping was identified as belonging to a maid who worked for a Dr Ruxton. Ruxton's wife and maid had gone missing and he confessed to the crime. The case remains a landmark in forensic identification.

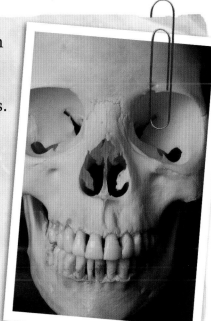

THE JOAN BENT CASE

In 1986, Joan Bent's frozen, strangled corpse was found in the trunk of her car. She had eaten potatoes for dinner. In the opinion of Dr Michael Baden from the office of New York City's Chief Medical Examiner, the food had been digested for only half an hour. Her husband had already stated that she ate two hours before leaving for work and going missing. The forensic evidence prompted him to change his story and offer a confession to her murder.

THE BLACK WIDOW POISONINGS

In 1989, North Carolina resident Pastor Dwight Moore collapsed after eating a pastry given to him by his new wife. Baffled by his symptoms, doctors ran a toxicology screening and found he had 20 times the lethal dose of arsenic in his system.

When police looked into the past of his wife, Blanche, they discovered that her boyfriend, Raymond Reid, had died of a mystery ailment. His body, along with those of Blanche's former husband, father and mother-in-law, were exhumed and examined. Elevated levels of arsenic were found in the hair and nails of all. In 1990 Blanche Taylor Moore was convicted of the murder of Reid and sentenced to death by lethal injection.

GLOSSARY

accumulate To gather or collect something.

builder's lime A powder made from limestone used as a hardener in mortar and plaster.

cartilage Firm, flexible connective tissue found in the human body, especially the throat.

cell nucleus A part of the cell containing DNA and responsible for growth and reproduction.

cerebral hypoxia A serious lack of oxygen to the brain.

decomposition The breakdown of the body after death.

dismember To remove the limbs from a human or animal.

dissection Making a detailed examination of body parts by cutting them apart.

embedded To be fixed firmly and deeply in a tissue mass.

exhumation Digging out a buried body.

fire warden A look-out posted to watch for parachute-dropped firebombs during World War II.

John Doe An unidentified victim.

post-mortem After death.

post-mortem examination An autopsy carried out on a body after death, to determine the cause of death.

putrefaction The process of rotting in a dead body.

quicklime A strong powder made from limestone, used to dissolve dead bodies in grave sites.

Renaissance The blossoming of art and science in the 14th - 16th centuries.

residue Small amount of poison that remains when the main dose has broken down.

rigor mortis The stiffening of the limbs in a body after death.

scam artist A cheat, swindler, or fraudster.

superimpose To place something on or over something else.

systematically To carry out something according to a fixed plan.

FOR MORE INFORMATION

ORGANISATIONS

American Academy of Forensic Sciences
410 N 21st Street
Colorado Springs, CO 80904
USA
(719) 636 1100
Website: http://www.aafs.org

The British Association for Forensic Odontology (BAFO)
Dental Centre
JSU Northwood
Sandy Lane
Northwood
HA6 3HP
Website: www.bafo.org.uk

FOR FURTHER READING

Cooper, Chris. *Forensic Science* (Eyewitness Books). London: Dorling Kindersley, 2008.

Evans, C. *The Casebook of Forensic Detection: How Science Solved 100 of the World's Most Baffling Crimes.* London: Wiley, 1998.

Frith, Alex. *Forensic Science.* London: Usborne Publishing Ltd, 2007.

Hopping, Lorraine Jean. *Autopsies and Bone Detectives* (Crime Scene Science). Tunbridge Wells: Ticktock Media Ltd, 2007.

Joyce, Jaime. *Toe Tagged: True Stories from the Morgue* (24/7: Science behind the Scenes: Forensic Files). Danbury, CT: Children's Press, 2007.

INDEX